I'm Grateful for You

Congratulations on purchasing this journal and taking the first step to making your personal world and relationships, as well as the world of someone you love, a happier place. For ideas, visit http://pgshriver.com/gjournals.

Entry Suggestion:

Think about the person to whom you plan to gift this journal, then each day think about an aspect of that person for which you are grateful (ie: their smile, their encouragement of you, their coffee making skills, or anything you appreciate about them) and begin writing and/or drawing on the next page. For more suggestions, visit pgshriver.com/gjournals.

Date:

Today, I am so grateful for you because-

Date:

Today, I am so grateful for your-

Date:

Today, I am so grateful for your-

Date:

Today, I am so grateful for your-

Today, I am so grateful for your-

Date:

Today, I am so grateful for your-

Date:

Today, I am so grateful for your-

Date:

Today, I am so grateful for your-

Date:

Today, I am so grateful for your-

Date:

Date:

Date: /

Date:

Date:

Date:

Date:

Date:

Date:

Date:

Date:

Date:

Date:

Date:

Date:

Date:

Date:

Date:

Date:

Date:

Date:

Date:

Date:

Date:

Date:

Date:

Date:

Date:

Date:

Date:

Date:

Date:

Date:

Date:

Date:

Date:

Date:

Date:

Date:

Date:

Date:

Date:

Date:

Date:

Date:

Date:

Date:

Date:

Date:

Date:

Date:

Date:

Date:

Date:

Date:

Date:

Date:

Date:

Date:

Date:

Date:

Date:

Date:

Date:

Date:

Date:

Date:

Date:

Date:

Date:

Date:

Date:

Date:

Date:

Date:

Date:

Date:

Date:

Date:

Date:

Date:

Date:

Date:

Date:

Date:

Date:

Date:

Date:

Date:

Date:

Date:

Date:

Date:

Date:

Date:

Date:

Date:

Date:

Date:

Date:

Date:

Date:

Date:

Date:

Date:

Date:

Date:

Date:

Date:

Date:

Date:

Date:

Date:

Date:

Date:

Date:

Date:

Date:

Date:

Date:

Date:

Date:

Date:

Date:

Date:

Date:

Date:

Date:

Date:

Date:

Date:

Date:

Date:

Date:

Date:

Date:

Date:

Date:

Date:

Date:

Date:

Date:

Date:

Date:

Date: